the absent TEACHER

LESSONS I LEARNT FROM MY FATHER

DWAIN AWAI

THE ABSENT TEACHER: Lessons I Learnt from My Father

For information contact:
Dwain Awai
www.successjourney.info

Book and Cover design | Editing
DHBonner Virtual Solutions, LLC
www.dhbonner.net

ISBN: 978-0-692-17500-2

Printed in The United States of America

This book is dedicated to the one
who hurt me the most...
My Father

"**Your destiny lies before you.** Not behind you!"

~Keith Awai

CONTENTS

Acknowledgments

There are so many people I would like to thank, who have not only been supportive of me on my success journey, but have also been vital and instrumental to both my growth and personal development. Unfortunately, I cannot list everyone; however, to all of you who I have encountered on my way to releasing this story, please know how much you have inspired and motivated me to keep going and not quit.

"Thank you!"

But truly, it is the following to whom I owe my deepest gratitude... for being my rock, my reason, and my "why" in making *The Absent Teacher* a reality.

First, I want to thank God. For without Him, His blessings, and His grace, nothing in my life would have been accomplished.

Next, I owe my everything to my mother, Monica! She has always been my number one supporter and foundation. I am forever grateful for the prayers, the patience, and the unconditional love she has given me throughout my entire life. She really is a superwoman and my main inspiration. *Thank you* over and over, Monics, for never giving up on me, and for being both Mom and Dad to Cristal and me.

I would also like to thank my sisters, Cristal and Kella, and my niece and nephew, Keriese and Christian, for being my primary motivation in becoming the best that I can be. You don't even know how important you have been for me; to make you proud and eventually provide for you financially is a lifetime goal I am confident I will achieve!

I would also like to thank my beautiful girlfriend, Allison, who has been exceptionally supportive of this entire process and journey to becoming the best me. Sometimes, not even fully understanding my vision, she smiles and says,

"I believe in you!" That is truly all a man can ask for.

I would also like to thank those I have highlighted in this book for having such a defining impact on my life: Dr. Walter (RIP), Dana, Brent, Clint, Marlon, and Jason (RIP). Also, my boys back home from on the block in St James... *thank you, fellas!* You guys were there for me during some of the lowest points in my life and did not even know it! Forever grateful to each one of you—blood for life!

And to Ms. Desireé Harris-Bonner, for believing in my vision for the book, being patient with my crazy mind throwing out a million ideas all at once, and for providing great advice and direction for the project; all while transforming a painful story into one of hope and inspiration. To you, I am forever grateful!

And last, but not least, I want to thank "The Absent Teacher" himself, my father, Keith Awai (RIP). None of this would have been possible without your lessons and our experiences. I am sorry that our last conversation probably did not go the way you wanted it to. At that time, I was just not ready. But, I understand now... and you are forgiven. I guess I can say that you are my hero because I would not be the man I am today—and the man I am becoming—if it were not for your actions, or the lack of.

I love you man... and I miss you! We did it!

Introduction

He met her while coaching tennis at St. Joseph's Convent; an all-girls school in Arima, the second largest of three boroughs in Trinidad and Tobago; which was an area located on the easternmost coast.

Two years older than she was, and extremely handsome, all the girls wanted to be with him.

And why wouldn't they? At only 18, he was the local *hot boy*. Nevertheless, she was content just hanging out, hiking, going to the beach, and partying with their small group of friends. She wasn't going to chase him.

Still, some years later, they would marry, and she would give birth to me. Yet, before I would see my first birthday, he would be gone. And so began my instruction in the course of life, from my first teacher... my father.

"The Absent Teacher," is an instructional memoir highlighting five primary qualities I've gained in my life, and now demonstrate, due to experiences with my father; not so much because he embodied them, but because of the very fact that he did not.

Even more so, it's a testimony of the reality that one can indeed become all they were created to be, in spite of not having positive examples modeled before them; for it is a truth that we can learn as much from the mistakes and failings of others as their successes and victories. And, that we can decide for ourselves to go through the process of achieving our highest dreams, even if we have to choose to do things differently than those we love most.

Throughout this book, I will share pieces of my story... his story... our story, in the hopes that you will also be encouraged to do better; to be better.

Recognizing for yourself, that even in their absence, our fathers can teach us great lessons that we can embrace and impart to our children, our families; and those we have been graced to serve and work with, our communities.

Truly, *"The Absent Teacher"* has been written with the singular goal of helping you to step beyond what happened (or didn't happen), past unrealized expectations, through that space of acceptance, into a place of forgiveness.

Why?

So that you can move forward and manifest the vision and goals you have for your life, your home and relationships, and your businesses and careers.

While sharing the lessons I've learnt from my father, I don't just speak to you about the characteristics of integrity, responsibility, acceptance, community, and forgiveness from the comfortable position of one who hasn't personally experienced the struggle, testing, and trials necessary to fully manifest these attributes in my life.

Not at all.

Instead, I liken myself more to that of a tour guide than

a travel agent, walking with you on this journey to becoming the best version of ourselves.

Therefore, I hope that as you read the following pages, *"The Absent Teacher"* will become more than just a book to you. I pray that it will become a source of encouragement; a manual or guide you can use to navigate and maneuver to that area of extraordinary growth.

Let's begin.

1 integrity

"Integrity is keeping a commitment

even after circumstances have changed."

-David Jeremiah

Integrity, as a concept, is defined as the **"consistency of actions, values, methods, measures, principles, expectations, and outcomes,** and in ethics, it is regarded as **"the honesty and truthfulness or accuracy of one's actions."**

In other words, it is the quality of remaining true to oneself and others, by firmly upholding one's core values and principles.

Your word is your bond...

Integrity derives from the Latin word *integer*, which means whole and complete. Therefore, integrity inherently possesses a sense of 'wholeness' and consistency of character. When you are operating with integrity, others will easily be able to witness a congruency between what you say and what you do. And, when you are 'whole' and consistent, you won't say one thing, while your decisions, behavior, and actions are saying something else.

You exemplify this characteristic by being reliable and doing what is 'right,' regardless of the consequences.

* * *

"Integrity is doing the right thing,
even when no one is watching."

-CS Lewis

* * *

This was not the case with my father. From the time he and my mother separated, it seemed as if he had also separated himself from my sister and me, ceasing to be an active presence in our lives, and continuously going back on his promises to us. Married to my mother for about three years, my father walked out of our house and began a new life with a new family.

Although I would have loved to have had a close relationship with him, it was nearly impossible to do. Not because there weren't plenty of opportunities available to support one, but because he was not consistent with initiating interactions. And even when he did, I could not depend on him to follow through or keep his promises.

For example, Keith would often take me to different fields to watch him play both soccer and cricket, or get me and my sister to go to Macqueripe Beach with my step-sisters. However, this sort of behavior was not consistent with what I would have hoped for, he would tell us in one breath, *"I'll come pick you guys up and take you to the beach,"* and by the next breath, he would not show up. In some cases, he would call to cancel, but this still did not remove our feelings of disappointment.

In addition to this, Keith wouldn't attend any parent-teacher meetings, only came to one of my soccer games, and didn't participate in other important life events.

If you were to ask him about this shortcoming, he would excuse it by expressing to us that it created tension in his new home for him to spend time with us.

Or, he would blame his lack of integrity on the fact that he and his brothers had pretty much ended up growing up on the streets, staying with his friends most times due to his father's abusive behavior toward his mother, saying that, *"My mother was not around,"*, *"I grew up hard,"* or, *"I don't know how to love."*

Now, the story (as it's been shared with me), was that one day my grandfather had beaten my grandmother so badly that she had to leave, packing up and taking her youngest son, my Uncle Tony, with her. Her goal was to make her way to safety and come back for her other sons once she had gotten settled. Apparently, my grandfather returned and over time, instilled into the boys the lie that their mother didn't care about them... she had left them, so it must be true, right?

Soon, my grandfather got into a new relationship and was also quite abusive to her as well; eventually driving my father and uncles to leave the house to live with friends and wherever they could find to lay their heads at night, as they no longer wanted to remain in such an unhealthy environment.

Thus, my father grew up hating his mom, never speaking to her again, even unto her death.

Nevertheless, integrity is a characteristic that shows up *in spite* of one's circumstance or situation. It is not exhibited because everything is perfectly aligned, but many times, when things are in disarray and extremely inconvenient or uncomfortable.

EXEMPLIFYING INTEGRITY

- From my father's example, I have endeavored to demonstrate the character of integrity in every area of my life. And, because I do not feel as if he did his due diligence to take care of us, I am committed to getting into a position that will eventually allow me to take care of my mom, my sisters, my niece, and my nephew... no matter what.

My adherence to this level of commitment has potentially cost me relationships and personal material comfort; sacrificing so that I can save for their future.

- It is my goal to consistently do what is right by others and provide support to not only my friends, but even strangers, whenever I can; giving back to those less fortunate and in need. I also make time to mentor others, such as past employees of Enterprise Rent-A-Car, by giving financial and personal development advice and sharing my experiences, challenges, and victories to inspire them.

LESSON 1: INTEGRITY

- It is important to me to always stand up for what I believe is right. At Enterprise (in the past), and even now at FedEx, my peers can confirm that I am one 'who speaks his mind' and stands strong for what I believe. Often, it leads to my getting into a bit of trouble.

Once, at Enterprise, my Area Manager, Dan, visited my office and said to me, *"Dwain, we are not here to fight principle battles."* However, I couldn't agree with him. As Les Brown says, "Stand up for what you believe in, because you can fall for anything."

A ROLE MODEL FOR INTEGRITY

Dr. Walters was one of my secondary school teachers. We first crossed paths when I was in Form 3, which is a defining high school year in Trinidad—and throughout the Caribbean—because it is at this stage that you "choose your subjects." Much like in the United States, where you pick your major or the field you would like to pursue into adulthood; such as business, languages, arts, science, etc.

At any rate, by the time Dr. Walters came to Trinity College as a Geography teacher and my form teacher, I was already categorized as a troubled and unruly student. By this time, I had probably been suspended from school more than five or six times for various reasons. Despite this reputation, Dr. Walters took it upon himself at every opportunity he could find to speak to me about character, reputation, consequences of actions, responsibility, and being a man. I'm not sure if he had kids of his own, but he certainly took an interest in studying and knowing me.

One thing he would always say to me, or like we would say in Trinidad, always giving me these prayers (meaning 'always nagging'), was, *"Awai, a true gentleman wears a hint of jewelry and dress and carry themselves with class!"*

He would preach this to me time and time again because one of the rules I would break was the dress code. Like, wearing a printed shirt under my white school shirt so that you could see the print underneath, wearing my shirt collar flipped up, wearing baggy pants, or a big Spanish-link gold chain with a big diamond cut 'D' pendant; which back then you wore to complement your Nikes, Jordan's, or name brand earrings that you would be sure to take off before school, but put right back on the way home.

Now, the reason why he is such a great example of integrity to me is that despite my disrespectful demeanor and the fact that other teachers were not fans of me, he believed he could positively influence me.

Disappointment after disappointment, suspension after suspension, he still held true to his goal of being a positive role model in my life, without altering his perception of me.

What stood out was his true commitment to my success the time I was expelled during the first term of Form 5 (my senior year). Although the event that occurred was more a small brawl involving many students than a massive fight, I was seen as the instigator; causing the Ministry of Education to label me as being "unfit to be amongst students." As a result, they did not want to allow me to take my final CXC exams, which were necessary for me to get my diploma.

Dr. Walters really put his career and reputation on the line for me, going against the Principal's instructions by writing a letter to the Minister of Education, pleading for a pardon to allow me to take the exams and, in his words, *"Not spoil the future of this young man!"*

After a joint meeting with the school officials, my mother, and Dr. Walters, the pardon was granted; however, I was required to report to the Principal's office to be signed in and out by my mom, both before and after exams.

Throughout the remainder of that school year, Dr. Walters would again keep his commitment and word to my mother and me, by helping me to prepare for exams. He sent daily assignments home with my cousin and took the time to call some evenings to check on me to see if I had any questions. The outcome of this effort was that by the end of the school year, I had earned two 1's (with distinctions; which are like A+'s), two 2's (which are like B's), two 3's (which were C's)–and thankfully, only one F.

None of which could have been accomplished without his commitment to stay true to his promise of helping me develop, regardless of possible consequences; such as a lack of popularity amongst his peers, or even the possible loss of his job due to his sending me material without permission from the Ministry of Education or the Principal.

Rest in Peace, Dr. Walters. I wish you were here now to see who I have become. You would be proud. And, oh yeah, I now wear a hint of jewelry and dress with class!

END OF CHAPTER EXERCISE

What does integrity mean to you? Which characteristics best define the quality of integrity for you?

LESSON 1: INTEGRITY

Go back and review what you just wrote.

After reflection, be honest with yourself... Do you possess these characteristics? Are you consistently demonstrating these qualities, and if not, what can you do to improve in this area?

THE ABSENT TEACHER

2 responsibility

*"It is not **only for what we do** that we are held responsible, but also for **what we do not do.**"*

-Moliere

Responsibility, as defined by Merriam Webster, is the **"the state or fact of having a duty to deal with something; being accountable or answerable for something or someone.** It is something you should do, not just because it is legally required, but primarily because it is morally right.

So, let's look at responsibility from two aspects:

- *The duty to take care of something or someone*
- *The state or act of being accountable for something within one's power or control*

In either case, my father would receive an "F" if this were a graded course. Looking at the first aspect of "the duty to take care of something or someone," my father did not fully fulfill his due diligence of this. Yes, he paid child support of TT750 ($125) the first of every month (which by the way was for two children. Clearly, not enough).

However, part of his duties as a father was also to *be present*; especially for important events such as award ceremonies, football games, swimming competitions, etc.

Now, don't get me wrong. I fully understand that once my parents separated, he now had a new family and a new life. Yet, we (my sister and myself) were still his children... his responsibility. Their divorce, for whatever reason, did not change this reality.

LESSON 2: RESPONSIBILITY

* * *

"The ability to accept responsibility

is the measure of the man."

-Roy L. Smith

* * *

For the second aspect of "being accountable for something within one's power or control," I could never fully accept his claim of *"I don't know how to love."* This is something I had heard him say hundreds of times, in different interactions, until I spoke with one of my father's brothers and a best friend of his from childhood because I wanted to understand more about his upbringing.

You see, although I grew up extremely close to the maternal side of my family, I have never met my paternal grandparents. Or, at least if I did, I don't have any memory of it, nor did my father never spoke of them with me.

Everything I have ever heard about them, I learned through my mother's recollection of things.

Still, beyond sharing with me that Keith didn't have

much of a relationship with his parents, she didn't have much else to tell me.

I don't believe this is because she didn't want to share information with me. I believe she didn't know anything more. This was probably a result of my father keeping his pain buried deep within himself; only using hints and self-deflecting side comments; like the times he would say to me, *"Dwain Awai"* (to this day, I am not sure why he would always call me by my full name), *"No one never gave me nothing. My mother and father never gave me nothing. I made it by myself!"*

When it comes to Keith taking responsibility for HIS life and actions, it was evident from his words and actions that he struggled tremendously.

He could not dig himself out of a "victim" role.

Though he presented himself as a bold, confident, and tough person to friends and colleagues, I now realize that he was a broken, traumatized soul; tormented by his inability to deal with situations head-on and fully experience life until his death.

LESSON 2: RESPONSIBILITY

Now don't get me wrong, in no way was Keith weak or a pushover! In all other aspects, he showed immense strength; especially when he took on other demons which haunted him, such as a serious drug addiction, which in reflection, was a type of a mask he hid behind, an escape for him from his past experiences.

He just could not seem to be able to apply that same willpower to overcome his trauma of "feeling neglected" by my grandmother; a perception he never challenged, even unto the day of his death. Still, perception is your reality unless you challenge it!

* * *

"Responsibility finds a way.

Irresponsibility makes excuses."

-Gene Bedley

* * *

EXEMPLIFYING RESPONSIBILITY

So, yes. I give him an "F" for this. Because, despite his upbringing, Keith could have chosen to take ownership and hold himself accountable for not doing the same to me! A decision to act differently from what he had grown up seeing would have gone a long way in breaking the 'Awai curse.' Instead, by not doing so, he simply allowed the same sense of abandonment and neglect he had experienced as a boy and young man to be directly passed to me.

Yes, I still had my mom, and no, I did not grow up in an abusive home like he did, but the emotional pain that had been inflicted resulted in my spending more than two decades lashing out at the world. I lashed out at anything, or anyone, that invoked a feeling of rejection or challenged my sense of worth!

And, man, was I violent!

However, as time went on, I began to realize that one of the lessons I learnt from my dad was that just because we have experienced heartbreaking situations or faced devastating circumstances, it is still our responsibility to address issues, hurt, and any residual brokenness head-on; taking action, not repeating those same behaviors or misplacing our anger and harming others.

This is not to say that I am not sometimes disappointed by, pained, or even angered at the actions of others which seem unjust or ill-willed, but I am learning that the responsibility for how I respond rests with me. I can't control them, *but I can control me and my actions.* Therefore, I have decided to take the residual effect of Keith's actions and break the cycle by committing to never abandoning my family and friends, finding a way to do what I say I am going to do, and making myself accountable to those I love for those things within my power or span of control.

A ROLE MODEL FOR RESPONSIBILITY

Back in 2005, I was in Central Florida, doing an internship at Polk County School Board. One day, someone heard me speaking and because of my accent asked, *"Where are you from?"* As soon as I replied that I was from Trinidad, the person said, *"Hold on a sec. Somebody else who works here is from Trinidad. Let me get her."* A few minutes later, a lady came around the corner, speaking loudly, *"Where? Him?"*

After approaching me... *"You from Trinidad?!"*

"Yes."

Excited, she said, *"My mother is from Trinidad. Let me call her."*

That was my introduction to Dana. It was the beginning of a bond that endures to this day, with her mother quickly becoming my "Mom in America" who sends me authentic cooked Trini food, which I devoured daily! In the years that followed, Dana and Moms were nothing less than angels sent from heaven to help me throughout my journey in the United States.

One key act of kindness, which stands out most amongst their 26 zillion acts of kindness toward me, was Dana deciding to sponsor me for my green card. This decision meant taking on all financial obligations for me while I went through my process to become a permanent resident.

This was important to me, not just because I needed someone to function in this role on my behalf or the U.S. Government would have denied my application, resulting in my dreams of being able to stay in the States and making a better life to be lost. But, she did it without my asking, offering to do it simply because she believed in me.

She did not owe me anything. In fact, she already had enough on her plate. As a widowed, single mother, she is the sole provider in her family, designated to handle all of the business dealings for her mother and brothers, all while raising her son alone and managing a full-time job as the Director of Payroll, which often required more than 60 hours a week.

Also, over the years, Moms had begun to lose her eyesight, and in the past year became legally blind. So, even after a long day at work, Dana is still needed to address Moms care, as well as the care of the household.

Now, what you don't know is that Dana has two adult siblings in Chicago. My thoughts, which I have shared with her, were that this wouldn't be such a weight if these men would periodically come down to Florida to assist with Moms' care. It seemed so unfair.

Dana's response?

"Awai, I am doing my part to help my mother. I cannot worry about what others are doing or not doing. I can only do my part because I will have to answer to God. And, so do they."

Dana exemplifies "responsibility" and demonstrates an outlook about the task she has taken on that I admire and want to embody as I commit to care for my family, as this is the true example of responsibility—one I wish my dad had understood; that regardless of his upbringing, his experiences, his issues, that he would want "to do his part" in raising his children... all of them.

But, as Dana said, I will do my part because I will have to answer to God. And, so does Keith!

END OF CHAPTER EXERCISES

What goals, people, or passions motivate you to get up every day and push through? Write down your top 3 'whys' and remember that your 'why' should be something bigger than you.

1.

_____

_____

_____

2.

_____

_____

_____

3.

_____

_____

_____

For those who are visual: *Create a vision board.* Resurrect that arts-and-crafts-kid in you, get a blank board (could be your favorite color), and glue pictures of your 'whys', goals, or passions that you would like to achieve, or people who inspire and motivate you.

Try to be well-rounded and post things that reflect every area of your development; such as, materialistic things you may want to acquire, goals you want to achieve in your professional career, or things you want to achieve in your personal life and relationships, etc.

Here is an example of mine:

3 acceptance

*"**Truth** never pleads or compromises or wavers.*

*It invites and awaits your **acceptance**."*

-Vernon Howard

Acceptance, simply put, **is embracing the reality of a situation.** More importantly, it is taking any situation or circumstance for what it is... not trying to change it or figure it out. It is synonymous with **recognition, realization,** and **acknowledgment.**

Many people reject this quality, because sometimes, to accept something painful gives the impression that you are in agreement with what was done, and the person who harmed you is getting off scot-free. Acceptance is difficult when you're not happy about what it is you're receiving... or having to accept.

But, the truth is, there is a great freedom in just letting what is, be what it is—or what was, be what it was.

* * *

"What we resist we persist."
-Carl Jung

* * *

When we resist or reject a certain reality, rather than recognize it for what it is, it brings even greater discomfort; which is what I repeatedly experienced in the situation with my dad. I had so much anger and hatred toward him, and a deep desire for things to have happened differently, that the negative aspects of it were becoming a large part of the man I was developing into.

Keith chose to neither "accept" nor "embrace" his

childhood experience. Instead, he resisted it and used it as a scapegoat for his own bad behavior.

Therefore, by not identifying the factors causing his pain, he moved through life as a victim of his circumstance; always defensive and not realizing that he was persisting in passing down the same poor experience to others.

You see, what you think of most is what you become or attract. Proverbs 4:23 reminds us of this, *"Be careful how you think; your life is shaped by your thoughts,"* (GNT). My dad focused so much on how his dad had been abusive, how his mom had 'abandoned' him, and how unfair things had been for him, that it shaped his life.

He then manifested the same in his actions.

For example, at his job at Angostura, where he worked in management, he would often say how unfair it was that the company would bring in these young "green" boys for him to train, and then they would become his boss.

Now, it was probably true, and if so, yes, it was unfair. However, because of the way he allowed it to define his thought process, it created such a huge chip on his shoulder.

A chip so big that he was considered an "ignorant" (ignorant meaning lack of self-control in the Caribbean) person, which may have likely interfered with some of his upward mobility in the company.

Please, don't get me wrong. Hats off to the man, as he still had a very successful career at Angostura; especially when you consider his background growing up.

He achieved much more than was expected for someone overcoming what he had. I don't even think he realized how much he accomplished. But, he focused so much on the glass being half empty that he never recognized the portion of his glass that was full. He never accepted what was—and make the adjustments necessary to move beyond it—so that he could enjoy it.

EXEMPLIFYING ACCEPTANCE

I have also suffered from that mindset, only recently realizing that the world is not out to get "Dwain Awai." This was my illusion of my own making, and had I accepted the reality of my life earlier, my learning curve could have been cut in half, saving me a lot of trouble in life. It took me more than 30 years to understand one simple, yet complex, theory: that, in most cases, we have a choice in whether we will embrace, or reject, the situation or circumstance.

One of the most powerful prayers that I have read is called the *Serenity Prayer*. I have a copy of this prayer both in my car and on the wall in my dining room as a reminder, and I read it daily. There is a longer version of it, but most of us are acquainted with this portion:

"God grant me the serenity to accept the things
I cannot change; courage to change the things I can;
and wisdom to know the difference."
-Reinhold Niebuhr

Now, just because you accept a situation, it doesn't mean that you are in agreement with what was done, that you support the action, or that you have accepted that things will be this way forever. All you are doing is acknowledging the true issue, the root cause, of your pain or discomfort so that you can either find a solution or remedy. Or, in my case, develop a healthy strategy to cope with the hurt and neglect.

Much like going to the Doctor, when you visit the office or clinic, you come in with some sort of malady or issue, right? However, once the Doctor identifies the cause of the concern, he is able to prescribe a remedy, whether it be a procedure, medicine, or rest.

It is also important to note that acceptance is a process. Like the medication or period of rehabilitation following a procedure, there is a process you must go through to get back to a heathy state.

You have to work at it.

* * *

"The healthy man does not torture others,
generally it is the tortured who turn into torturers!"

-Carl Jung

* * *

LESSON 3: ACCEPTANCE

I could not change my dad's behavior, but I could change the way I allowed it to affect me. I could choose, like Keith, to move through life as a victim, blaming him for my inability to love and connect with others in a healthy way, or I could use my pain and experiences as motivation to help someone else; accepting the reality of what had happened and deciding for myself what type of man I was going to be.

Hence, my writing this book.

A ROLE MODEL FOR ACCEPTANCE

Brent is a great friend of mine. As a matter of fact, he is more like the big brother I never had.

I have known Brent for almost my entire life. Despite his being five years older than me, we played in the same football club, the Ken Elie Football Coaching School for soccer, and then went on to attend the same high school. But, where the real friendship formed was when Brent helped me get into Concordia College in Selma, Alabama.

Brent helped me to get into the school by putting in a

good word with the soccer coach at Concordia, who signed me as a freshman player and offered me a scholarship.

During my freshman year at CC, Brent took me and the younger guys under his wing, guiding and mentoring us. And, even though I only attended the college for one year, before transferring to Warner University (formerly Warner Southern College) in Lake Wales, Florida, he continues to be my guide and mentor.

It is truly the many early morning and late-night talks with Brent that have helped me overcome many of the struggles I've encountered since being in the States.

The reason he is the perfect example of acceptance is because he is always open-minded, looking on the brighter side of things, with a clear, composed mindset even when things are chaotic or confusing. Like this one time when things really did become dark for him, yet despite being afraid and not fully understanding what was going on, Brent kept his wits, remained composed and positive, and most importantly, faithful in the belief that God would bring him through it all. It is in this situation that he had an epiphany and his true vision was manifested.

One morning, he woke up and could not see.

Not a thing.

I learned about it when I called him that morning and he answered not sounding completely like the Brent I knew. Immediately, I sensed that something was wrong and after asking how he was doing, he shared with me what was going on. I was extremely worried for him, and while I was asking him, *"Shit! What are you going to do? What do you think happened?"* Brent calmly said, *"I don't know. But, I'll go to the doctor and I will be okay. This won't defeat me."*

And, it didn't.

The following is his recap of what happened:

> "Woke up one morning and realized that I was not seeing out of my right eye, which is my better eye. I thought that it was allergies, so I took some allergy tablets. When that didn't clear it, fear began to set in and my life goals seemed to fade... just as my eyesight had.

I went to the optometrist to check it out and he said that it looked like I have a hole in my eye. Panic rose up because this was unexpected *and* scary!

The next day, I went to a specialist who diagnosed my situation as Central Serous Retinopathy, or CSC (*a condition where fluid accumulates under the retina, causing detachment and vision loss*). The doctor suggested surgery, with a three-week recovery. I asked the doctor if it can heal on its own and he said, 'yes', but it will take six months to heal.

I then told him that I would go the natural route because I believe I can heal faster. He said that I should come back in one month to let him know my final decision on whether I wanted surgery or not; his tone indicating that in one month I'd be requesting surgery because of the discomfort of the situation.

LESSON 3: ACCEPTANCE

At that point, my faith, belief, and determination to prove him wrong took over and I began to live out my saying that *sometimes life can take away your sight from you in order for you to see your vision.*

When I went back to the doctor after 30 days had passed, he asked, "Are you ready for surgery?" I said, "I feel much better."

After reviewing my test results and seeing a big improvement, he was in awe, agreeing that surgery was not required and that I should heal naturally.

I was then scheduled to return to his office in two months, at which time he cleared me to resume all activities as normal and stated that he could not believe that I was able to heal in such a short period in comparison to other people who was diagnosed with this condition."

Although Brent was dealing with a traumatic situation, rather than falling into a 'poor me' mindset, his acceptance of the reality of the situation allowed him to be composed and clear-minded. He was open to seeking out possible solutions; resulting in a positive outcome and a new and improved insight on life.

END OF CHAPTER EXERCISES

To truly have acceptance, we must dig deep and face those underlying feelings and address "what is happening?" "Is it factual?" "What emotion are we really feeling (anger, sadness, etc.)?" "Who, or what, is making us feel that way?" "What may we have done to cause this behavior or pain?"

If the answers are something you can do to change the situation, then you change it. If there is nothing you can do about the circumstance, then accept it for what it is at the time, and work on modifying the way you are reacting to it; whether this means addressing the issue head-on or releasing the inner turmoil and making peace with it.

On the lined pages that follow:

1. Describe a situation that you are resenting or not accepting. It could be a person, place, or thing.

2. Identify if it is factual or a possible illusion attacking something deeper. Here you have to be very honest and have a true gut check. Is this really happening or bringing up a similar feeling or memory from a past experience?

3. What feeling(s) or emotion(s) are you experiencing? Again, be honest with yourself.

4. Determine what (if any) role you played to cause this reaction, circumstance, situation, etc.

5. Is a resolution within your control? If yes, what action steps will you take? If no, how will you modify the way you are reacting to the issue, so that you can arrive at a place of peace... and acceptance?

LESSON 3: ACCEPTANCE

THE ABSENT TEACHER

4 community

*"We don't **heal** in isolation,*

*but in **community**."*

-S. Kelley Harrell

When we refer to community, we are specifically talking about your **inner circle of influence, your support group,** those individuals you can **turn to, depend on, laugh with, or cry with.**

These are your accountability partners, a select group of people who share common beliefs, interests, and goals.

Having the right circle of influence is so important.

As a matter of fact, surrounding yourself with the right people is one of the keys to success. And when I say "right", I mean those who genuinely care about your progress and well-being, and vice versa.

This person, or group of people, is a complement to you, not competition. And remember, community does not have to only be comprised of close friends and family; it can also include a mentor, counselor, therapist, teacher, etc.

You see, where Keith went wrong was that he kept so many things he was dealing with to himself, trying to fix everything on his own, and as a result, did not benefit from a system of checks and balances. There was no one to provide him with wise counsel to consider or to help him see his own blind spots.

His claim of, "I did it all on my own and no one never gave me anything!" although potentially being true, came at a great expense to his health, his sense of peace, and his relationships.

It is extremely possible that had he trusted and confided in others, even seeking professional support, he might have been able to come to terms with the losses and abandonment in his past, taken advantage of opportunities to understand more about his mother's situation, and discover productive ways to deal with his pain; instead of resorting to drugs, gambling, and extending the same cycle of loss and abandonment to his children.

* * *

"Alone we can do so little;

together we can do so much."

-Helen Keller

* * *

Even in his final letter to me, he stated *"there is so much I would like to say to you, but some things should be left unsaid."* Evidently, allowing himself to be open and vulnerable to discussing his true feelings was too difficult.

One can only believe that it was a defense mechanism he employed to protect himself from his deeper pain and the sense that to share would expose him to judgment or being seen as weak.

We will never know the fullness of what he kept buried deep within himself; however, for those of us who knew and loved him, like my own mother and stepmother, they chose to cover for him, rather than help him uncover; thinking that they were helping him, when in reality, they were hindering him.

I don't blame them.

Still, this is exactly why you must make sure that your support team and accountability partners hold your feet to the fire. That their love for you doesn't cripple you. That their love for you is greater than their fear of how you will respond.

Your community will be honest and trustworthy. It will be your safe place; one where you can show the ugly parts of your being, and be washed and healed. They will not enable you to deteriorate to the worst part of what you can be, but support you in becoming the greatest version of who you are.

LESSON 4: COMMUNITY

It is the place where you can be not only transparent, but also vulnerable. And yes, these terms are two different things. Where transparency means that you allow others to "see" what is going on with you, vulnerability means that you also allow others to "touch" your issue in an effort to resolve it. So, as healing is indeed a process, both transparency and vulnerability are necessary in that process.

EXEMPLIFYING COMMUNITY

Due to my experience with my father, I have learned how important it is to have the right folks around you. Whether during the lowest periods of my life where I was overwhelmed with sadness and anger, or the highest seasons where joy and thankfulness were in abundance, I can honestly say that my support group was there to check me and help me put things into perspective, as well as cheer me on and celebrate with me. The hurt I carried, due to my dad's absence, taught me this lesson and prompted me to create that supportive structure in my life.

You see, throughout my life—from early childhood into my present—I sought the help of therapists and counselors to manage my pain and anger. Nevertheless, nothing seemed to change or improve.

As a matter of fact, in some cases it seemed to get worse. I would find myself becoming angrier and more resentful of my father (and even myself) for not being able to "man up" and deal with "a little pain," as I had convinced myself that it was. Now as I think about it, I realize that the reason my many visits to the counseling couch did not work can be narrowed down to these three points:

1. The primary reason I didn't achieve the benefits of counseling was because I was not attending because "I" wanted the help or that "I" saw value in it. I went to please my mother. She told me to go, so I went. And, although she understood the importance of these sessions, I did not!

Even though I showed up, I still possessed a mental block towards therapy, as I felt as though this stranger could not possibly know what I have been through.

2. The second reason counseling did not work for me initially was because I would not open up during the sessions, and as I mentioned earlier, I would display neither transparency nor vulnerability. How could they help me or understand my issue, if I wouldn't be real with them?

3. The third and final reason was a result of the first two reasons. In the past, I never took the time to listen carefully to absorb the information being shared with me. Nor would I implement and execute the next steps or actions presented to me.

I learnt these three keys are critical to recovery, growth, and sustainability: You have to be willing to be open about your situation, you need to take action on the wisdom and counsel provided, and you must want to do it for yourself.

And, let me tell you, it's a process! A long, drawn-out, challenging, humbling, embarrassing, painful process.

It's not going to be easy... but, it will be worth it.

Even today, I face difficult moments when I want to give up and revert to the old, angry, violent me again. That old version of me comes out from time to time, but what is important is that I am aware of it. I embrace the fact that I am human and continuously work to correct it. However, none of this could be possible if I didn't remain accountable to my community—sharing what I am feeling, receiving feedback provided, and acting on it—when I have a setback, or as my sister Cristal refers to it, have "a human moment!"

* * *

"You can't heal

what you never reveal."

-JayZ

* * *

LESSON 4: COMMUNITY

This was something my father was not fortunate to understand; therefore, I cannot fault him for not doing something he did not know.

So, share your thoughts, pains, and experiences with your support group, because it will help you overcome your issues, or at least find a healthy way of coping with it; remembering to be there for them as well. Someone needs *your* support to help *them* to work through *their* challenges.

Isn't that what friends are for?

A ROLE MODEL FOR COMMUNITY

In the previous chapters, I shared a few of my accountability partners. People who have supported me with their wisdom, insight, and ability to be exceptionally honest with me—helping me to see situations from a different perspective—even if it meant having to confront my ego and feelings.

Still, one ride or die confidante, that one person willing to "ride" any problem out with me, or "die" trying, is my cousin, Clint. With just one-year difference between us, we grew up together, both in the fact that we lived within ten minutes of each other and that we attended the same primary and secondary schools, as well as some sports, like cricket.

As you know, when boys grow up close to one another, they tend to get into trouble together, and we were no different. We would lie to our parents and grandmother to protect one another and fight for (and against) each other.

Clint, along with his younger brother, Khellon, were more like my brothers than cousins. We have a sense of loyalty and commitment to one another that has spanned well into our adulthood. Therefore, they have both been a strong part of my community since we were kids, and we have held each other accountable toward our success.

From the time we made an oath that we would become millionaires by the time we hit our thirtieth birthday (a mark we haven't quite hit... *yet*), we have continued to keep one another focused on maintaining that drive and moving toward that goal; to follow in the footsteps of our maternal grandfather, Milton (aka Shark), who—although we had not met—we greatly admired.

See, our grandfather had created a legacy of providing for his family. With very little education, he was still able to create a business that allowed him to not only care for his children, but also his children's children. So much so, that the fruits of his labor are still being enjoyed today, even though the company is no longer in existence.

* * *

"A good man leaves an inheritance

to his children's children."

~Proverbs 13:22a (ESV)

* * *

Like him, we wanted to be able to "take care" of each other and others in the family. To that end, we have always had an instinct to "hustle;" to make money.

We automatically functioned as each other's system of checks and balances. And, though we do not always agree with decisions or actions made, we always respect one another, never taking the opinion or criticism personally.

We knew that it came from a place of love.

Today, Clint runs and owns an extremely successful business in Trinidad with his wife Nikki, and we still speak to one another several times a day, bouncing ideas off of each other, discussing challenges, sharing good news, or even talking "shit" to keep ourselves motivated, uplifted, and grounded. This, despite our living in two different countries.

We even take annual vacations together to connect in the same physical space to reminisce on our childhood, acknowledge each other's accomplishments, and to refine next steps on our goal, both individually and collectively.

I have been fortunate to be blessed with someone in my life who has some of the same aspirations that I do, and is willing to help me face my shortcomings, while strengthening me in the areas where I am weak. Clint can identify, with pin-point accuracy, the source of the challenge I may be facing and support me in being able to "look at the picture outside of the frame."

LESSON 4: COMMUNITY

Together, we make a dynamic, unstoppable, team.

Why? Because, as we say to one another, it is not "I make it, or he makes it. It's *we* make it!" And, we will not quit until our goal has been reached, our family cared for, and a legacy has been left for generations to enjoy!

END OF CHAPTER EXERCISE

Think of two goals for each of the following categories that you would like to achieve within the next 12 months to ensure a balanced life:

1. Health
2. Family
3. Finance
4. Fun

Next, do a deep analysis of the people in your current circle (this can include family, friends, coworkers, etc.) who you believe can support you in achieving these goals, either through holding you accountable, mentorship, or being an example. Then, ask them to partner with you.

If you cannot think of anyone in your immediate circle, take your search to the Internet, Universities, or Programs for mentors who can assist you.

Key things to note:

The person (or persons) you have chosen should be reliable, honest, and straightforward with you. And, you must be open to receive feedback, recommendations, and critiques from them.

Also, your goals need to be specific, measurable, relevant to your specific journey or process, and attainable (be realistic).

Then, after reviewing your results for the first 12 months, expand on your goals—take it up a notch—for the next 12 months in the same categories and review annually.

THE ABSENT TEACHER

LESSON 4: COMMUNITY

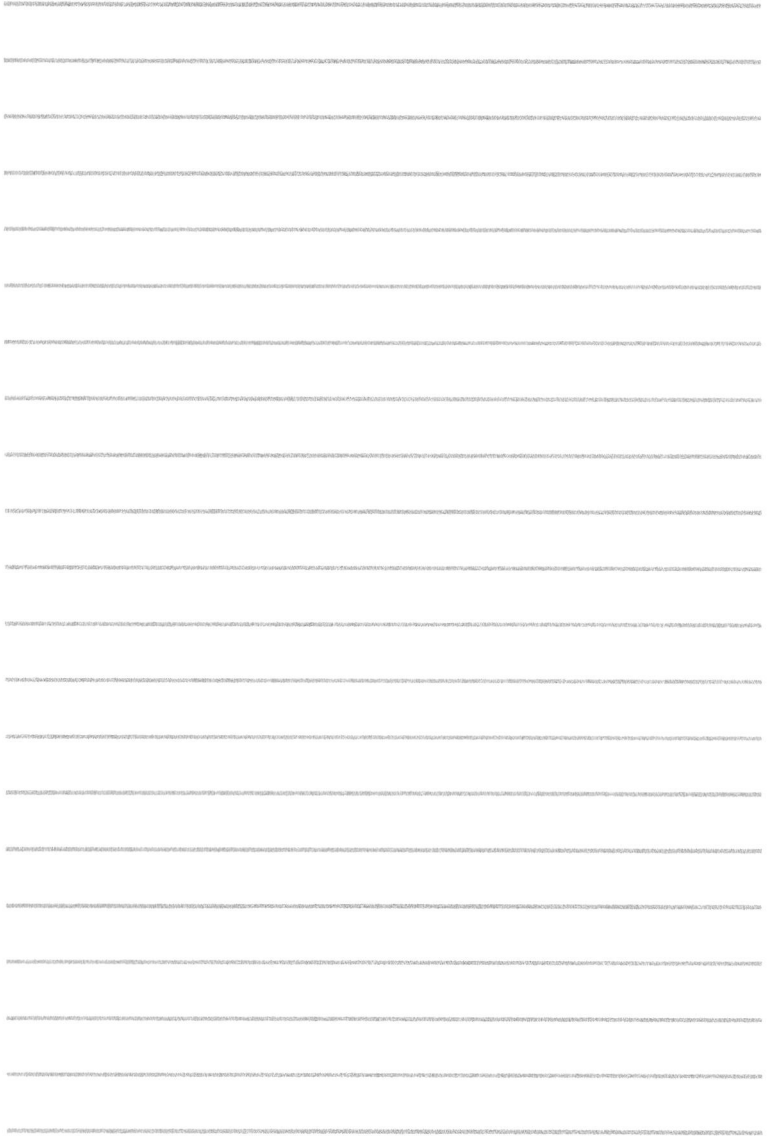

5 forgiveness

Forgiveness is giving up the hope

That the past could have been any different."

-Oprah Winfrey

Forgiveness is defined as the **act of releasing someone from a debt owed.** It essentially means to **pardon** or **excuse** someone (even ourselves) **from blame** for an injustice or misdeed. It is a decision to move past a wrong and cease to harbor ill-will or resentment about an offense.

Interestingly, it is also synonymous with words like clemency, absolution, and mercy; meaning that it is a conscious, deliberate choice to not exact vengeance or demand payment from a person or group who has caused harm, regardless of whether they deserve your forgiveness... or not.

Many times, an offender will find it easy to ask for (or demand) that the injured party quickly grant forgiveness; generally throwing out a surface *"I'm sorry"* while subsequent behavior or action hasn't yet demonstrated a depth of comprehension that they have grievously hurt someone.

Or worse, they may simply go on about their business as if nothing has happened; leaving you to work through an exhaustive list of emotions, such as: anger, hatred, sadness, regret, resentment, disgust, betrayal, and pain.

When these emotions—which we typically associate as negative—show up, it is natural to want to fight back, get even, or hold the offender's feet to the fire.

To make them pay.

LESSON 5: FORGIVENESS

And, due to our wanting to prove that we are not weak, we tend to hold on to grudges and withhold forgiveness until we feel that they have been punished enough... thinking that we are "getting back at" or "making it even" with them, when in fact we are not harming the other person at all. The truth is, we are giving them more power by keeping ourselves imprisoned by the initial wrong.

Although he did not write it, there is a quote made famous by Nelson Mandela, who—over time—came to forgive an entire nation of evils against himself and other South African people: *"Resentment is like drinking poison and waiting for your enemy to die."*

This is something I believe my father had difficulty understanding. Though I know he honestly attempted to do so before he died, by asking me to forgive him, he did not recognize that the underlying issue was the lack of forgiveness he held in his heart toward his own parents for their wrongs and lack of care of him! Remember, as mentioned earlier, "what you resist, you persist." Well, let's add to that: "What you resist, you persist... *and often duplicate!*"

By my father not forgiving his parents for what he perceived was wrong, he ended up duplicating and passing along to others. Because he held onto the negative effects of the painful emotions for more than 50-something years, most likely up until his sudden death, he—not his parents—robbed himself of the peace and tranquility that he desired yet was so absent throughout his life.

Therefore, the cycle was not broken. By retaining this pain, it created such a clouded vision and depth of bitterness that he was not even cognizant of how his actions caused pain for those who loved him dearly... and for me.

* * *

"When you forgive, you in no way change the past — but you sure do change the future."

-Bernard Meltzer

* * *

LESSON 5: FORGIVENESS

EXEMPLIFYING FORGIVENESS

Trust me, I know this is a tough pill to swallow because I have struggled with this for over 35 years, and still wrestle with it from time to time even while knowing that what I am telling you is true.

The saying, "The sins of the father is passed onto the son," despite not being truth in the eyes of God because He said that He will judge each of us individually for our actions, in earthly terms—in my case—rang true.

I was repeatedly duplicating Keith's rage, hatred, and resentment. Anyone who I felt "trespassed" against me, I vowed to make it even, and held onto the wrong until I made it so; robbing myself of that very peace and tranquility my father had longed for and allowing it to eat me up like a cancer.

Then, one morning around 4 a.m., I received a call with the news that my father had passed away. I remember the one-minute conversation like it was yesterday.

It went like this:

My phone rang. I looked at it and it was my father's number. Ignoring the call, I thought, *this man is crazy calling me at 4 or 5 in the morning!*

The phone rang again, and my girlfriend at the time said, "Dwain, who is that?" I responded, "My dumb father. I don't know why he is calling at this hour!"

I ignored the call again. It rang a third time, and highly aggravated now, I answered, "Yea!!!" However, the voice on the other end was not him; it was his girlfriend. She said, "Dwain." I responded, "Yes."

"It's aunty Helga here." (In the Caribbean, as a sign of respect, you call adults "aunty" or "uncle" despite not being blood-related.) I responded, "Yes." She then said, very calmly before hanging up and not waiting for my response, "Your father died this morning."

LESSON 5: FORGIVENESS

I remember turning back over and lying there, confused and trying to process the information; my girlfriend asking, "What he want?" Calmly, I responded, "It wasn't him. It was his girlfriend and she said he is dead." Jumping up, she screamed a series of questions I couldn't yet answer: "What?!" "How?!" "Are you ok?! Is your sister ok?! Call your sister. Call your mom!"

Stunned, I continued lying there for about 20 minutes or so, before finally reaching out to my sister, who was crying hysterically by the time I called; saying, "Dwain! Dwain! Daddy dead!"

Again, still not knowing what to say, I think I responded by asking, "How? Do you know? It will be okay."

Then, I hung up the phone and went back to sleep.

You see, I had no feelings for this man, so I did not shed a tear when he died, nor did I attend his funeral. I honestly did not cry until a couple of years ago when I realized that I was even more angry at him once he was dead, than I had been when he was alive.

In error, I thought that once he died, my anger and hate towards him would have died with him, because he was no longer here. However, instead of dissipating, the pain grew because I felt that any opportunity to rub my success in his face—now that he was gone—had been stolen from me.

That's when it hit me that my issue was not about him, it was about me! I was just like him because I had duplicated what he had done. I had not forgiven him for his wrong-doing before he died, much like he had not forgiven his parents for their wrong-doing before they died. And, I was still bitter like he had been after they died.

It was then that the realization came that something had to change, and that the problem was within me.

So, for the ten years following his death, I began the journey to forgiveness of my father; not for him, but for my own healing, which I can honestly say I did on November 20, 2017. I remember the date, which I now consider to be my new birthday because it was on that day that *a new Dwain* was born, and everything started to un-fold for me in life, like writing this book.

LESSON 5: FORGIVENESS

* * *

"True Forgiveness is when you can say,

thank you for that experience."

-Oprah Winfrey

* * *

The great news about forgiveness is that it's not really about the person who harmed you. Yes, it does embody the by-product of freeing the perpetrator, whether they remain unrepentant, are in denial, or—like my father—no longer living. But, at a deeper level, the one who forgiveness truly frees... *is you.*

And keep in mind, forgiving someone does not mean that what they did to you was okay or that you would let them hurt you again. Forgiveness does not mean forgetting, nor does it mean allowing or excusing offenses.

It just means that you are aware that by carrying the burdens of non-forgiveness, you hurt yourself more.

It takes a high level of mental and emotional energy to maintain aggression and hostility toward another person.

Therefore, once the emotional debt is cancelled, we free ourselves from the past, from the prison of painful memories and situations, and from the need for everything to be "even" before we can move on and live our best life. The key to the liberty we seek is within our own hand.

However, it is a process; no one will master the art of forgiveness in one day because as humans, we react to pain through our emotions. Still, it is counter-productive to continue hurting ourselves by holding on to the injury, and then passing that pain onto others.

And, although there isn't a prescribed timeframe for extending forgiveness, there is a natural progression from injury to healing to wholeness. As it is with the natural healing process, so it is with the emotional one.

To not move through this natural healing process only invites further damage to our peace, well-being, and growth.

LESSON 5: FORGIVENESS

A ROLE MODEL FOR FORGIVENESS

Anyone who knows me from growing up back home, especially in my early teen years, will not just think of me or mention my name without also mentioning Marlon or Jason. We were always, and I mean always, together! We did nothing without each other and were really and truly that example of brotherhood you hear about on hip-hop songs and see in old school mafia movies.

We would really ride-or-die for one another! And, we dated the same group of girls; meaning, if I had a girl I liked, that girl had to make sure she had two other friends for Marlon and Jason or vice versa. Let's not even go there with doing something to one of us because you can guarantee the three of us will be coming for you... and we did.

It did not matter where you were, it was on! Not in any form or fashion am I supporting violence, but that was the bond we had; like the musketeers, *it was one for all and all for one!* Fast forward some years later, what we thought would never happen, happened.

Aside from everything we had been through together and our brotherhood, an incident occurred where my high school girlfriend confronted me with some information that I knew she could have only gotten from either Marlon, Jason or one of the other guys on the block, but she said it was from Jason.

Being young, and with an ego through the roof, a discussion between Jason and me never occurred and the "team" broke up. Well, more like I split from Marlon *and* Jason because I felt Jason had done me wrong and Marlon was aware of it, yet said nothing to me.

With my perception as my reality, I felt betrayed!

Fast forward again a couple years later, I left Trinidad for college in America, still not talking to my boys! Then, one day I received a call from a friend back home. "Dwain, they killed your cousin last night!" Shocked, I asked, "Who cousin?" The reply? "Dog. Jason!"

My heart sank instantly, because I instantly knew that I would never have another opportunity to reconnect with him and put the past behind us. What hurt even more was the fact that numerous people had pleaded with me to talk with Jason and work things out: my father, my sister, my mother, and mutual friends. However, due to my stubbornness, I purposely neglected to do so, because I did not realize then that it was not about approving of his actions; it was about releasing the anger and resentment toward my boys and our growing and learning from it.

I remember one perfect moment that I could have extended the gift of forgiveness. It was an early morning while I was on vacation in Trinidad and preparing to head back to the airport. When stopped at a red light, there was a guy crossing the street in front of me.

The guy was Jason.

My windows were down, so he recognized that it was me. He actually stopped to look at me, and I looked right at him; knowing that I wanted to say something to him or even give him a ride home, because it was close to his house, and from his countenance I knew he wanted to say something as well. But again, our egos got the best of us, and as I drove off he turned around and walked away.

That was the last time I saw Jason. If I had known that would have been my last opportunity to speak with my boy, I would have. However, that's the thing, we never know if we will get another chance! After that, I made it my business to reconnect with Marlon and make amends. In spite of our not being as close as we had been growing up, Marlon will always be my boy and I believe he feels the same way about me; and I also know that Jason is looking down smiling on us both!

Only recently have I forgiven myself for not making things right with Jason while he was here, and I know that I will forever carry him in my memory and my heart!

R.I.P. J.

I miss you man...

* * *

"It's one of the greatest gifts you can give yourself,
to forgive. Forgive Everybody."

-Maya Angelou

* * *

END OF CHAPTER EXERCISE

On a piece of paper, write a list of everyone who you believe has done you wrong and forgive them. Then, either reach out to them to reconnect or move forward, knowing there is no malice. Now, not everyone is going to be willing to sit down and have a conversation, but that is okay. Remember, this is more for your peace of mind and letting go of a burden than their acceptance of your journey to peace and forgiveness.

If reconnection isn't possible, consider getting a helium balloon—or a couple, depending on how long your list is— and writing their name on it with a marker.

Don't forget to include a balloon with your name on it, too.

Next, go to one of your favorite places; a place that brings a sense of peace or tranquility for you. This could be a park, the beach, or a mountain. Ask God to grant you strength to forgive, and then release the balloon(s); watching it float away as a symbol of all the pain, anger, resentment, hate, etc.

Repeat throughout life as necessary!

THE ABSENT TEACHER

The Final Lesson

There is a lot of controversy around the cause of my father's death. The autopsy said he died from a heart attack, yet some believe that he was either poisoned or that it was a brain aneurism.

Due to this, a second autopsy was recommended; however, his wife, my stepmother, had chosen not to pursue it so that the she could get everything over with, have him buried, and move on with her life and begin the healing process.

No, I did not go back to Trinidad for the funeral because again, I was so angry with him. At the time, I was fine with this decision, as I didn't have a relationship with him; especially not one strong enough that made it worth my time... or expense.

Not only that, during this season, I was still going through the process with immigration for my green card and did not want to risk my future in the United States by leaving it. The truth is, I didn't really care for him.

My father's wife paid the costs for the funeral but decided not to purchase a headstone because she had been extremely hurt by Keith. Therefore, my sister reached out to me to pay for one.

Again, I said *no*.

So, being creative, she marked a tree to note its location.

However, some time later, I visited his burial site. Or, at least the area where we thought he was buried, since the marked tree had since been cut down. To this day, although we have an idea of the location, we don't know exactly which plot my father is buried in as there is no marker.

Which pretty much sums up Keith's entire existence. His death was just like his life... unsettling and without peace.

In spite of it all, I know my father believed in God. I just don't think he had the needed patience for himself and God's plans to bring him to the place of peace he so longed for before he left this realm. You see, if Keith had done so, then I believe he would have eventually found what he called, in his own words, *"a place to call Home!"* Nevertheless, I thank him for the lessons I learnt, even in his absence, and I look forward to continuing the learning process, while taking advantage of every opportunity to share it with others.

So, here we are.

It has been a journey moving from *there* to this space of understanding; and although I know that each of us has a different story, a separate path, it is a truth that the five keys I have learnt through what I have experienced in my relationship with my father—Integrity, Responsibility, Acceptance, Community, and Forgiveness—once realized and implemented, can help you move beyond any situation you have experienced, are currently experiencing, or may experience in the future.

The final lesson then, which is the foundation upon which the previous lessons function, is to work through it with patience and faith! Both of these qualities are critical along the journey to extraordinary growth and success.

See, *without faith in God* and *having patience in the process,* it will be extremely difficult to manifest fruit from the seed that has been sown. You'll give up long before you see His perfect purpose fulfilled in your life.

So, thank you for choosing to read *"The Absent Teacher"* and as I have shared my father's story—my story—our story, I pray that you were able to discover something you can make use of along your success journey. I appreciate your allowing me to be transparent with my story to enlighten yours!

And to you, Keith... *Dad.* I am now finding my own place to call home, and I look forward to sharing our story to help others break through their shackles of the past and move forward toward freedom! Because yes, there is freedom in the realization that although we aren't responsible for the wound, we are indeed responsible for our healing.

I'm still working on that...

Dad, the Awai curse is now officially broken! Relax now and Rest in Peace! You are home.

ABOUT THE AUTHOR

Dwain Awai was born on the beautiful, tropical island paradise of Trinidad where he lived until the age of 19.

In 2001, after earning his high school diploma, Dwain migrated to the United States to attend college.

Dwain has ten-plus years in the sales and customer service industry where he has excelled due to two main characteristics: a strong ability to build genuine relationships with his customers by earning their trust and loyalty *and* a determination to never give up, which if he is asked, "why are you so persistent?" he will respond, "my family is depending on me! I am all they've got!"

With a life-long obsession to find "peace" within himself and "forgiveness" of his Dad for leaving him and not being there to help him navigate the transition into "manhood,"

Dwain sought the help of several counselors, behavioral therapists, and close friends and family.

As a result, Dwain has decided to embark on a new journey to empower others with similar experiences, so that they can also discover the treasures of peace and forgiveness, in order to fulfill their true purpose on earth.

To that end, Dwain is currently working on releasing a series of books outlining his story and the lessons he has learnt. He is currently available for speaking engagements, workshops, and empowerment programs.

To connect with Dwain, visit:
www.successjourney.info